A BRIEF INTRODUCTION

TO BITTENSOR

-

AI & BLOCKCHAIN:

THE NEXT BIG THING?

Murat Durmus

Murat Durmus

Imprint: Self-Published

ISBN: 9798871414590

Cover Image:
Murat Durmus - Bittensor Logo (https://bitten-sor.org/resources/)

About the Author

Murat Durmus is CEO and founder of AISOMA (a Frankfurt am Main (Germany) based company specializing in AI-based technology development and consulting) and Author of the books " The Cognitive Biases Compendium" and "Beyond the Algorithm: An Attempt to Honor the Human Mind in the Age of Artificial Intelligence"

You can get in touch with the author via:

- LinkedIn:

- E-Mail: murat.durmus@aisoma.de

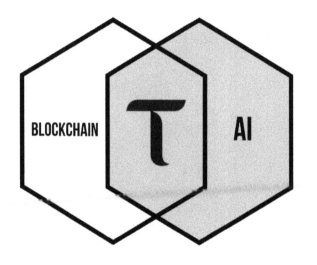

BLOCKCHAIN   AI

Note:

This book was written with the support of AI. Specifically, I created a custom GPTs (based on GPT4) called "Bittensor Guide." I fine-tuned it with only trusted documents regarding Bittensor content, including the Bittensor website, the corresponding whitepaper, and the GitHub repository. The content was checked for correctness, and I adjusted where I thought it made sense.

PREPARE TO BE PART OF A
CONVERSATION THAT WILL SHAPE
THE NARRATIVE OF TECHNOLOGY
FOR YEARS TO COME.

WELCOME TO THE FUTURE

-

IT'S JUST BEGINNING -

~

MURAT DURMUS

PREFACE

In an era where technological advancements are not just innovations but catalysts of change, the fusion of Artificial Intelligence (AI) and blockchain technology represents a frontier of untapped potential. This book, aims to demystify the complex interplay between these two revolutionary technologies, focusing on the role of Bittensor.

Bittensor, an ambitious project at the crossroads of AI and blockchain, is more than just a technological advancement; it is a paradigm shift. Its vision of a decentralized AI network challenges the traditional, centralized approaches currently dominating the tech industry. Bittensor is not just a concept but a tangible pathway to a future where AI is more advanced, equitable, and accessible.

It is a gateway for those curious about the potential synergies between AI and blockchain. Whether you are a seasoned technologist, a computer science student, an investor in cutting-edge technology, or simply a curious mind eager to understand the future landscape of AI and blockchain, this book is designed for you.

Through the following chapters, we will embark on a journey to explore the genesis of Bittensor, delve into its technical intricacies, and speculate on its potential to redefine the way we think about AI and blockchain. The objective is not just to inform but to spark a more profound interest and understanding of a topic that shapes the future of technology.

As the world stands on the brink of a new digital era, Bittensor represents a beacon of possibilities. Its story is one of innovation, challenge, and the relentless pursuit of a future where decentralized AI transforms the blockchain landscape. "A Brief Introduction to Bittensor - AI and Blockchain: The Next Big Thing?" is a guide to understanding this transformative technology and its place in the broader narrative of technological evolution.

Welcome to a journey into the heart of one of the most exciting developments in the modern technological panorama. I hope you enjoy reading it.

Murat Durmus

THE EVOLUTION OF AI AND BLOCKCHAIN

Chapter 1 sets the foundation, tracing the historical development of AI and blockchain, and leads up to the introduction of Bittensor. It aims to provide context and build anticipation for the deeper exploration of Bittensor in the following chapters.

The Dawn of Artificial Intelligence

The journey of Artificial Intelligence (AI) is a tale of ambition, ingenuity, and relentless pursuit of a dream that has long captured human imagination - creating intelligence that parallels our own. AI's inception dates back to the mid-20th century, originating from the classical period of mathematical theory and early computing technology. Pioneers like Alan Turing and John McCarthy laid the groundwork, proposing machines that could not just calculate, but think.

The evolution of AI saw its winters and renaissances. From rule-based systems of the 1980s to the machine learning breakthroughs in the 21st century, each phase brought us closer to machines that learn, adapt, and make decisions. Today, AI is not a distant scientific concept but a palpable force driving innovation across industries, from healthcare to finance.

Blockchain: The Ledger of Trust

Parallel to AI's evolution, another revolutionary technology emerged – blockchain. Initially conceived as the underlying technology for Bitcoin, blockchain has grown beyond its financial roots. At its heart, blockchain is a distributed ledger technology (DLT) that provides an immutable, transparent, and decentralized method of recording transactions.

The genius of blockchain lies in its ability to establish trust in a trustless environment. By using consensus mechanisms, it ensures that each transaction is verified and agreed upon by a network, making it nearly impossible to alter recorded information. This attribute has made blockchain a harbinger of change in areas demanding transparency and security, such as supply chain management, voting systems, and identity verification.

The Convergence of AI and Blockchain

The convergence of AI and blockchain is more than a mere amalgamation of technologies; it is the fusion of potential. AI brings the power of advanced data processing and pattern recognition, while blockchain offers a secure, decentralized platform to share and record this data. Together, they open a realm of possibilities:

- **Data Security and Privacy**: With AI's increasing appetite for data, blockchain can provide secure and transparent ways to store and share this data, addressing privacy concerns.

- **Enhanced AI Models:** Blockchain can facilitate the sharing of data and models across various entities, enabling collaborative AI development without compromising data security.

- **Trust in AI Decision Making:** Blockchain's immutable record-keeping can provide transparent audit trails for AI decisions, building trust in AI systems among users.

- **Decentralized AI Marketplaces:** Blockchain enables the creation of decentralized marketplaces for AI algorithms and data sets, democratizing access to AI technology.

Bittensor: A New Chapter

In this fertile ground of technological convergence, Bittensor emerges as a path-breaking initiative. By leveraging the decentralized nature of blockchain to distribute AI computations, Bittensor is not just riding the wave of innovation but creating its own. It represents a new chapter in the story of AI and blockchain – a chapter where decentralized AI networks reshape our approach to data, computation, and intelligence.

Looking Ahead

As we delve deeper into the subsequent chapters, we will explore the intricacies of Bittensor, understanding how it embodies the confluence of AI and blockchain, and envisioning its role in shaping the future of these technologies.

UNDERSTANDING BITTENSOR

Chapter 2 provides an in-depth look at Bittensor, outlining its foundational principles, operational dynamics, and the potential impact it holds in the realms of AI and blockchain. The chapter also acknowledges the challenges involved and the solutions Bittensor offers, setting the stage for further exploration of its capabilities and implications.

Bittensor: Envisioning Decentralized AI

In a world where AI and blockchain have evolved parallel, Bittensor emerges as a groundbreaking fusion of these two realms. It represents not just a technological innovation but a philosophical shift in how we approach and harness the power of artificial intelligence.

The Philosophy Behind Bittensor

The core philosophy is decentralization, a principle central to blockchain technology. This approach challenges the conventional, centralized models of AI development dominated by tech giants. Bittensor envisions a world where AI is created, accessed, and improved upon by a distributed network of contributors, democratizing the development and benefits of AI technologies.

Operational Mechanics: How Bittensor Works

At its heart, it is a decentralized network that allows different nodes, operated by various participants, to contribute to and access AI functionalities. Here's how it fundamentally works:

- **Decentralized AI Services:** Contributors can run nodes that offer specific AI services (like data processing, model training, etc.). These services are accessible to anyone on the network.
- **Token-Based Incentives:** Bittensor utilizes its native token, the TAO, to incentivize participation. Nodes that contribute valuable services are rewarded with TAO tokens, aligning individual incentives with the network's growth.
- **Dynamic and Self-Regulating:** The network leverages blockchain technology for governance, with mechanisms in place to ensure the quality and reliability of services. Nodes are ranked based on contributions,

and higher-ranked nodes receive more significant incentives.

Bittensor's Unique Position

Unlike traditional blockchain projects focused on financial transactions or data storage, Bittensor aims to build a globally distributed neural network. This ambition sets it apart, positioning it as a pioneer in the intersection of AI and blockchain.

The Potential Impact of Bittensor

Bittensor's model offers several transformative possibilities:

- **Decentralized Intelligence:** By distributing AI across a global network, Bittensor could reduce the barriers to entry for AI development, allowing smaller players to contribute and benefit from AI technologies.
- **Resilience and Scalability:** A decentralized network is less prone to outages and bottlenecks, offering a more resilient and scalable infrastructure for AI services.
- **Innovation through Collaboration:** The open nature of Bittensor could spur

innovation as developers from around the world share, combine, and build upon each other's work.

Challenges and Solutions

While Bittensor's vision is compelling, it has challenges. Issues like ensuring the quality of contributions, preventing malicious actors, and maintaining efficient network operation are critical. Bittensor addresses these through blockchain's inherent security features and innovative governance mechanisms to foster a healthy and productive network.

The Road Ahead

As Bittensor continues to evolve, it stands at the forefront of a new wave of AI development. It's a bold experiment in creating a decentralized, collaborative platform for AI, and its success could redefine the landscape of AI and blockchain technologies.

THE TECHNOLOGY BEHIND BITTENSOR

Chapter 3 provides an overview of the technical aspects, explaining how it uniquely integrates AI and blockchain to create a decentralized network for AI development and deployment. This chapter is crucial for readers seeking to understand the technological underpinnings that make Bittensor a groundbreaking initiative in the AI and blockchain space.

Bittensor's Blockchain Backbone

Bittensor's technological prowess is anchored in its innovative use of blockchain technology. Unlike traditional blockchains that primarily focus on financial transactions, Bittensor's blockchain is engineered to facilitate complex AI operations.

- **Decentralized Ledger:** At its core, it utilizes a distributed ledger to record and verify all activities within its network. This ledger is not just a transactional record but a testament to the computational contributions of each node.

- **Smart Contract Functionality:** Bittensor extends the concept of smart contracts to encapsulate AI tasks. These contracts govern the interactions between nodes, ensuring that the services provided and received are accurately recorded and rewarded.

- **Consensus Mechanism:** To maintain integrity and trust within the network, Bittensor employs a unique consensus mechanism. This system validates transactions and evaluates the quality and value of AI services provided by the nodes.

The AI Dimension of Bittensor

The AI architecture is designed to be as decentralized as its blockchain framework. The network facilitates a distributed approach to AI development and deployment, wherein multiple nodes contribute to collective intelligence.

- **Distributed Neural Network:** The network operates as a global neural network, with each node contributing a part of the larger AI model. This structure allows for the parallel processing and development of AI functionalities.

- **Data Handling and Processing:** In its ecosystem, data is shared and processed across various nodes, ensuring robustness and diversity in data handling. This method enhances the learning and adaptability of the AI models.

- **Model Training and Deployment:** Nodes can train AI models using data available within the network and deploy these models for specific tasks. The decentralized nature ensures that these models are continually updated and improved by the collective efforts of the network.

Integrating AI with Blockchain

Integrating AI and blockchain is not just parallel but deeply intertwined. Blockchain provides a secure and transparent platform for AI operations, while AI enhances the efficiency and capabilities of the blockchain network. This synergy is evident in several aspects:

- **Security and Trust:** AI enhances the security mechanisms of the blockchain, while blockchain provides an immutable record of AI activities, building trust in AI operations.
- **Incentive Alignment:** AI contributions are incentivized through blockchain-based

rewards, aligning individual contributors' interests with the network's overall health.

- **Decentralized Intelligence Marketplaces:** It facilitates the creation of marketplaces for AI algorithms and datasets, leveraging blockchain for secure transactions and AI to offer sophisticated services.

Overcoming Technical Challenges

Bittensor's ambitious fusion of AI and blockchain is not without technical challenges. Issues such as network latency, data privacy, and the efficient allocation of computational resources are continuously addressed through innovative solutions and network upgrades.

A Technological Symbiosis

It represents a remarkable symbiosis of AI and blockchain, each enhancing the capabilities of the other. This chapter delves into the technical intricacies that make Bittensor a pioneering force in decentralized AI, setting the stage for a future where AI and blockchain are not just parallel advancements but collaborative forces driving innovation.

BITTENSOR'S ROLE IN THE FUTURE OF AI

Chapter 4 delves into the potential future impact on the field of AI, discussing its role in democratizing AI development, its societal and ethical implications, and the economic changes it might usher in. This chapter aims to provide a comprehensive view of how it could significantly alter the landscape of AI and what that means for the future.

The Paradigm Shift Towards Decentralization

Bittensor is more than a technological innovation; it's a harbinger of a new era in AI development. With its decentralized approach, this chapter explores how it is poised to redefine the future landscape of artificial intelligence.

- **Democratizing AI Development**: Traditional AI has been predominantly in the hands of a few tech giants. Bittensor disrupts this model by democratizing AI development, enabling a broader range of participants, from individual developers to smaller organizations, to contribute and benefit from AI advancements.

- **Fostering Collaborative Intelligence**: The network facilitates a unique form of collaborative intelligence. Unlike isolated AI systems, Bittensor allows diverse AI models to interact, learn from each other, and evolve collectively, leading to more robust and versatile AI solutions.

- **Global AI Network**: Envision a world where AI is not limited by geographical or organizational boundaries. Bittensor paves the way for a global AI network, harnessing worldwide computational resources and intellectual capital.

The Ethical and Societal Implications

The rise of decentralized AI networks brings forth significant ethical and societal implications:

- **Data Privacy and Security**: By distributing data processing across a decentralized network, Bittensor offers a potential solution to the growing concerns over data privacy and security in AI.

- **Reducing Bias in AI**: Decentralized AI networks can access more diverse data sets and computational perspectives, potentially de-creasing the bias inherent in current AI models.

- **Equitable AI Benefits**: Bittensor aims to ensure that the benefits of AI advancements are not concentrated in the hands of a few but are accessible to a broader community.

The Economic Impact of Decentralized AI

Bittensor's model has the potential to create new economic opportunities and paradigms:

- **New Business Models**: Decentralized AI networks will enable novel business models, allowing companies and individuals to offer AI services or share data in return for incentives.

- **Empowering Small and Medium Enterprises (SMEs)**: With lower barriers to entry, SMEs and startups can leverage advanced AI capabilities, fostering innovation and competition.

- **The Emergence of AI Marketplaces**: Bittensor could create decentralized marketplaces for AI models and datasets, revolutionizing how AI assets are traded and monetized.

Challenges on the Horizon

As with any pioneering technology, Bittensor faces its share of challenges. These include scaling the network to accommodate growing demands, ensuring the reliability and quality of decentralized AI services, and addressing regulatory and governance issues that arise in a decentralized setup.

A Forerunner in the AI Revolution

Bittensor is not just participating in the AI revolution but actively shaping its direction. By fostering a decentralized, collaborative, and ethical AI ecosystem, it is laying the groundwork for the future of AI. This chapter highlights Bittensor's potential impact and underscores the responsibility and opportunities that come with this transformative technology.

BITTENSOR AND THE BLOCKCHAIN ECOSYSTEM

Chapter 5 provides a look at how Bittensor fits into and interacts with the broader blockchain ecosystem. It compares it with other blockchain and AI initiatives, discusses the challenges it faces, and speculates on its future prospects and impact within the blockchain industry.

Bittensor Within the Broader Blockchain Ecosystem

As Bittensor carves its niche in decentralized AI, it's essential to understand its place within the larger blockchain ecosystem. This chapter explores Bittensor's interaction with existing blockchain technologies and its comparative position in this dynamic field.

1. **Synergy with Other Blockchain Projects**: It complements and enhances existing blockchain projects. Its focus on AI services adds a new dimension to the blockchain world, traditionally centered around financial transactions and data storage.

2. **Interoperability Challenges and Solutions**: Interoperability with other blockchains is critical for Bittensor to fully integrate into the broader blockchain ecosystem. The chapter discusses the technical hurdles and ongoing efforts to make it compatible with various blockchain networks.

3. **Blockchain for AI Beyond Cryptocurrency**: While blockchain is often associated with cryptocurrencies, Bittensor exemplifies how blockchain technology can be leveraged beyond financial applications, particularly in powering decentralized AI networks.

Comparative Analysis with Other Systems

It stands unique in its approach but shares the blockchain space with several other innovative projects. This section compares it with blockchain and AI systems, highlighting its distinctive features, advantages, and challenges.

- **AI on Blockchain – Different Approaches**: We examine how different projects integrate AI with blockchain, comparing their methodologies with Bittensor's approach.

- **Performance and Scalability**: A critical assessment of Bittensor's performance and scalability compared to other blockchain networks, especially in handling AI computations.

Future Prospects in the Blockchain Industry

- **Potential for Growth and Adoption**: Analysis of Bittensor's potential for growth within the blockchain industry, considering factors like technological advancements, market trends, and user adoption.

- **Innovation and Regulatory Landscape**: Discussion on how innovation in projects like Bittensor could influence the regulatory landscape of blockchain technology and AI.

Challenges in Integration

The integration of Bittensor into the existing blockchain ecosystem is challenging. These include:

- **Ensuring Network Security**: As it expands, maintaining the security and integrity of its decentralized network is paramount.

- **Regulatory Compliance**: Navigating the complex and evolving regulatory frameworks governing blockchain and AI technologies.

- **Community and Ecosystem Building**: Cultivating a robust community of developers, users, and stakeholders to foster an ecosystem around Bittensor.

A Catalyst in the Blockchain Revolution

It is not just a participant in the blockchain revolution but a catalyst, potentially changing how blockchain technology is perceived and utilized. By bridging AI with blockchain, it opens new frontiers for exploration and innovation. This chapter not only positions Bittensor within the current blockchain landscape but also envisions its role in shaping the future of this technology.

CHALLENGES AND OPPORTUNITIES

Chapter 6 provides a comprehensive analysis of the challenges and opportunities associated with Bittensor. It evaluates the technical, ethical, and regulatory hurdles it faces, while also highlighting the transformative potential it holds across various sectors. The chapter aims to present a balanced view of the risks and rewards inherent in its journey.

Understanding the Challenges

In integrating AI with blockchain, Bittensor encounters a unique set of challenges. This chapter delves into these complexities, offering insights into how they might be addressed.

1. **Technical Hurdles**: Integrating AI into a blockchain framework presents technical challenges, including network latency, data standardization, and ensuring efficient computation across decentralized nodes. These technical barriers require ongoing innovation and optimization.

2. **Data Privacy and Security**: While block-chain offers enhanced security, incorporating AI raises new privacy concerns, especially with sensitive data. Bittensor must navigate these concerns, maintaining data privacy without compromising the network's efficiency.

3. **Scalability and Resource Management**: It faces the challenge of scaling efficiently as the network grows. Critical concerns include managing resources in a decentralized environment, ensuring fair allocation, and preventing resource monopolization.

4. **Evolving Regulatory Landscape**: The regulatory environment for both blockchain and AI is still in flux. Bittensor must adapt to changing regulations while advocating for policies supporting decentralized AI innovation.

Exploring the Opportunities

Despite these challenges, Bittensor presents numerous opportunities for AI and blockchain and various sectors of the economy and society.

1. **Innovation in AI Development**: Bittensor's decentralized model opens up new avenues for AI development, encouraging collaborative and open-source approaches and accelerating AI innovation.

2. **Empowering Diverse Sectors**: Decentralized AI can revolutionize various industries, including healthcare, finance, and logistics, by providing scalable and secure AI solutions.

3. **Creating Economic Incentives**: Bittensor's token-based reward system creates new economic incentives for participants, fostering a community of contributors who are invested in the network's success.

4. **Promoting Ethical AI Practices**: By decentralizing AI, Bittensor has the potential to reduce biases inherent in AI models and encourage more ethical AI practices, contributing to the development of responsible AI.

Balancing Act: Risk and Reward

Bittensor's journey balances between navigating its challenges and capitalizing on its opportunities. This chapter discusses strategies that could be employed to mitigate risks while maximizing the benefits that it offers.

A Future Shaped by Collaboration

Bittensor stands at the intersection of challenge and opportunity. The way these are navigated will not only define the future of it but also shape the landscape of decentralized AI and blockchain technology. This chapter aims to provide a realistic yet optimistic overview of what lies ahead for Bittensor, highlighting its potential to drive collaborative and ethical AI development in a decentralized world.

GETTING INVOLVED WITH BITTENSOR

Chapter 7 is designed as a comprehensive guide for various stakeholders interested in getting involved with it. It provides actionable insights for developers, investors, businesses, and enthusiasts, outlining how each group can engage with and contribute to the Bittensor ecosystem. This chapter emphasizes the inclusive and collaborative nature of Bittensor, inviting a diverse range of participants to be part of this groundbreaking venture.

For Developers: Engaging with Bittensor

Developers play a pivotal role in the Bittensor ecosystem. This section guides developers interested in contributing to or utilizing the Bittensor network.

1. **Understanding the Bittensor Framework**: Familiarize yourself with Bittensor's blockchain and AI integration, as well as its APIs, smart contracts, and data protocols.

2. **Developing on Bittensor**: Steps to build AI models or applications on the Bittensor network, including setting up nodes,

contributing to model training, and deploying AI services.

3. **Community and Support**: Resources for developers, including forums, documentation, and community support systems, facilitating collaboration and knowledge sharing.

For Investors and Businesses: Exploring Market Potential

Bittensor presents new investment opportunities and potential business applications. This section is geared towards investors and businesses exploring its market potential.

1. **Investment Opportunities**: Analyzing Bittensor as an investment option, understanding its tokenomics, market trends, and long-term growth potential.

2. **Business Integration**: How businesses can leverage its decentralized AI network for their operations, from enhancing data analytics to deploying AI-driven solutions.

3. **Strategic Partnerships**: Opportunities for strategic partnerships and collaborations

within the ecosystem, fostering innovation and mutual growth.

For Enthusiasts and Visionaries: Contributing to the Future

It's not just for developers and investors; it's a platform for anyone passionate about the future of AI and blockchain.

1. **Educational Resources**: Learning materials for those new to blockchain or AI, providing foundational knowledge to understand and engage with it.

2. **Community Engagement**: How to get involved in the Bittensor community, including participating in discussions, attending events, and contributing to open-source projects.

3. **Visionary Contributions**: Opportunities for thought leaders, researchers, and innovators to contribute ideas and insights that could shape its future direction.

Joining the Bittensor Journey

Bittensor represents a collective journey towards a new AI and blockchain technology horizon. This chapter serves as a call to action for diverse groups to engage with it through development, investment, business applications, or community involvement. By joining the Bittensor ecosystem, participants contribute to this innovative project and become part of a movement shaping the future of decentralized AI.

OPEN MARKETS, OPEN OWNERSHIP

Chapter 8 focuses on the economic aspects of Bittensor, particularly its impact on creating open markets and promoting open ownership in AI. It addresses the economic opportunities and challenges presented by this new paradigm and discusses the broader implications for the future of business and technology. This chapter aims to provide an understanding of how it could transform the economic landscape of AI and blockchain technology.

The Economic Revolution of Bittensor

It is not just a technological breakthrough; it's a catalyst for a new economic paradigm. This chapter explores how its model of decentralized AI creates an open market and how it redefines the concept of ownership in the digital age.

1. **Decentralized Marketplaces**: It enables the creation of decentralized marketplaces for AI services and data. This section discusses how these marketplaces function, their advantages over traditional models, and the

opportunities they present for creators and consumers of AI services.

2. **Tokenization and Economic Incentives**: At the heart of Bittensor's economy is its token, the TAO. This section delves into how the TAO token incentivizes participation and contribution in the network, fostering a self-sustaining economic ecosystem.

3. **Impact on Traditional Business Models**: Its decentralized approach challenges and potentially disrupts traditional business models in the tech industry. This part analyzes the potential shifts in power dynamics, business strategies, and revenue models due to the advent of decentralized AI markets.

Open Ownership: A Paradigm Shift

The concept of open ownership is central to Bittensor's philosophy. This revolutionary idea redefines who owns and controls AI technologies and the intelligence they generate.

1. **Democratizing AI Ownership**: Bittensor's decentralized model diffuses the ownership of AI, ensuring it's not concentrated in the

hands of a few corporations. This section discusses the implications of this democratization for the AI industry and society.

2. **Collaborative Development and Ownership**: The collaborative nature of Bittensor's network leads to a shared development and ownership model. This part explores how this collaborative approach impacts the innovation process and the distribution of rewards.

Navigating Challenges in Open Markets

While its open markets and ownership model offer numerous opportunities, they also present unique challenges.

1. **Regulatory and Compliance Issues**: Decentralized markets operate in a regulatory grey area. This section discusses the regulatory challenges faced by Bittensor and the efforts to comply with existing laws while advocating for regulatory frameworks that support innovation.

2. **Ensuring Fairness and Quality**: Ensuring fairness and quality in a decentralized market is complex. This part examines the

mechanisms Bittensor employs to maintain quality and fairness in its open market.

Pioneering a New Economic Future

Bittensor is pioneering a new economic future with open AI markets and decentralized ownership. This chapter highlights its potential to reshape economic structures, democratize AI development, and lead a shift toward a more equitable and collaborative digital future.

CONCLUSION: THE DAWN OF A NEW ERA IN AI AND BLOCKCHAIN

A Journey Through the Bittensor Paradigm

This book embarked on an exploratory journey into Bittensor, a pioneering platform at the confluence of AI and blockchain technology. The chapters delved into the philosophical underpinnings, technical intricacies, potential impacts, challenges, and opportunities that Bittensor presents in this rapidly evolving digital era.

Bittensor: A Visionary Fusion

It stands as a testament to the power of visionary fusion – integrating blockchain's decentralization and security with AI's intelligence and adaptability. It challenges the centralized paradigms of AI development and proposes a new, democratized model where AI is collaborative, accessible, and equitable.

The Implications for Society and Industry

The implications of Bittensor extend far beyond the realms of technology. It promises to reshape economic models, democratize AI development, and introduce new paradigms in various sectors, from healthcare to finance. Its open market and ownership concept could redefine how we view intellectual property and collaborative innovation in the digital age.

Navigating the Challenges Ahead

While Bittensor offers a promising future, it navigates through a sea of challenges – from technical hurdles and scalability issues to regulatory uncertainties. Addressing these challenges requires technological innovation and collaborative efforts from regulators, developers, businesses, and the broader community.

The Role of Community and Collaboration

The success of Bittensor hinges on the strength and engagement of its community. This platform opens doors for developers, investors, visionaries, and enthusiasts to contribute to a burgeoning ecosystem that is shaping the future of decentralized AI and blockchain.

Looking Towards the Future

As we stand on the brink of a technological revolution, Bittensor emerges as a symbol of hope, pointing towards a shift towards a more decentralized, collaborative, and ethical digital future. Its journey is not just about technological advancement, but also about reimagining the potential of AI and blockchain in creating a fairer, more innovative, and inclusive world.

GLOSSARY OF TERMS

AI (Artificial Intelligence): A field of computer science dedicated to creating systems capable of performing tasks that typically require human intelligence, such as visual perception, speech recognition, decision-making, and language translation.

Blockchain: A distributed ledger technology that maintains a secure and decentralized record of transactions across multiple computers.

Bittensor: A decentralized network that integrates AI and blockchain technology, facilitating the creation, sharing, and improvement of AI models in a distributed manner.

Decentralization: The process of distributing and dispersing power or functions away from a central location or authority, often used in the context of blockchain networks.

TAO Token: The native digital currency used within the Bittensor network to incentivize and reward contributions to the AI models.

Smart Contract: Self-executing contracts with the terms of the agreement between buyer and seller being directly written into lines of code, primarily used on blockchain networks.

Tokenomics: The economics of a cryptocurrency, including factors like its distribution, supply, and how it can be used within its ecosystem.

Consensus Mechanism: A method used in blockchain networks to achieve agreement on a single data value or a single state of the network among distributed processes or multi-agent systems.

Distributed Ledger: A database that is consensually shared and synchronized across multiple sites, institutions, or geographies, accessible by multiple people.

Neural Network: A set of algorithms, modeled loosely after the human brain, designed to recognize patterns and interpret sensory data through a kind of machine perception, labeling, and clustering of raw input.

Data Privacy: The aspect of information technology that deals with the ability an organization or individual has to determine what data in a computer system can be shared with third parties.

Open-Source Software: Software for which the original source code is made freely available and may be redistributed and modified.

Peer-to-Peer (P2P): A decentralized communications model in which each party has the same capabilities and either party can initiate a communication session.

Interoperability: The ability of computer systems or software to exchange and make use of information; in blockchain, it refers to the ability of different blockchain networks to interact and exchange data.

Regulatory Compliance: Adherence to laws, regulations, guidelines, and specifications relevant to a business process or operation.

Tokenization: The process of converting rights to an asset into a digital token on a blockchain.

Scalability: The capability of a system, network, or process to handle a growing amount of work, or its potential to be enlarged to accommodate that growth.

Economic Incentives: Financial motivations for people to take certain actions, often used in the context of blockchain to encourage network participation and security.

REFERENCES

Bittensor's official white paper for a detailed under-standing of its technology and architecture:

"Bittensor: A Peer-to-Peer Intelligence Market"

https://bittensor.com/whitepaper

Bittensor Developer Documentation:

https://docs.bittensor.com/

Bittensor Project Github:

https://github.com/opentensor/bittensor

More Information:

https://bittensor.org/resources/

APPENDIX: PRACTICAL USE CASE EXAMPLE OF BITTENSOR: A DECENTRALIZED LANGUAGE TRANSLATION SERVICE

Overview

Let's consider a practical use case where Bittensor is utilized to create a decentralized language translation service. This service leverages the power of distributed AI across Bittensor's network to provide accurate and efficient language translation, rivaling traditional centralized translation services.

Step-by-Step Implementation

1. **Setting Up a Bittensor Node for Translation Services**:

   - **Hardware and Software Setup**: Users interested in contributing to the translation service set up Bittensor nodes. This requires standard computing hardware and an internet connection.

   - **Software Installation**: Configure Bittensor software from the official repository for language processing tasks.
     (https://github.com/opentensor/bittensor)

2. **Developing and Training Translation Models**:

- **Collaborative Model Development**: Developers across the Bittensor network collaboratively develop sophisticated neural network models capable of translating various languages.

- **Distributed Training**: The models are trained using a distributed dataset available on the Bittensor network, which includes diverse linguistic sources from nodes worldwide.

3. **Utilizing Bittensor's Decentralized Network**:

- **Parallel Processing**: The translation requests are processed parallelly across multiple nodes, enhancing speed and efficiency.

- **Data Privacy and Security**: Bittensor's blockchain backbone ensures that data privacy is maintained during translations, with no single point of data leakage.

4. **Providing Translation Services**:

- **User Requests**: Users send translation requests to the network, distributed among various nodes.

- **Real-Time Translation**: The nodes process these requests in real-time, providing accurate and swift translations to the users.

5. **Economic Model and Incentives**:

- **TAO Tokens as Payment**: Users pay for the translation services using TAO tokens, Bittensor's native cryptocurrency.

- **Earning Rewards**: Nodes contributing to processing translation requests earn TAO tokens in return, incentivizing participation and contribution to the network.

6. **Quality Assurance and Improvement**:

- **Continuous Learning**: The AI models continually learn and improve over time, using feedback and additional data from the network.

- **Community-Driven Quality Control**: The community monitors the quality of translations, ensuring high standards are maintained.

7. **Scalability and Expansion**:

- **Adding More Languages**: Over time, more languages and dialects are added to the service, broadening its scope.

- **Scalability**: As more nodes join the network, the service scales up, handling an increasing number of translation requests simultaneously.

Practical Benefits

- **Decentralization**: Unlike centralized translation services, this use case leverages a decentralized network, enhancing data privacy and system resilience.

- **Cost-Effectiveness**: Using a decentralized network potentially reduces operational costs compared to traditional centralized services.

- **Community and Inclusivity**: This model allows for a wide range of languages and dialects, including those not typically covered by mainstream translation services, fostering inclusivity.

- **Tokenized Economy**: TAO tokens create a self-sustaining economic model, incentivizing participants and users within the ecosystem.

Conclusion

This use case of a decentralized language translation service demonstrates Bittensor's potential in practical, real-world applications. It shows how AI and blockchain can come together to offer innovative, technologically advanced, economically viable, and community-driven services.

APPENDIX: A BRIEF HISTORY OF BLOCKCHAIN

While relatively recent, the history of blockchain technology is marked by several significant milestones and developments. Here's a more detailed look:

Pre-Blockchain Era (Before 2008)

- **Early Concepts and Cryptography:** The concept of a cryptographically secured chain of blocks was initially described in 1991 by Stuart Haber and W. Scott Stornetta. They envisioned a computationally practical solution for time-stamping digital documents so they could not be backdated or tampered with.

- **Further Developments:** In 1992, Bayer, Haber, and Stornetta incorporated Merkle trees into the design, which improved efficiency, allowing several documents to be collected into one block.

The inception of Blockchain with Bitcoin (2008-2009)

- **Satoshi Nakamoto's White Paper (2008):** The pseudonymous person(s) Satoshi Nakamoto published the white paper "Bitcoin: A Peer-to-Peer Electronic Cash System"[1], proposing a decentralized digital currency, Bitcoin.

- **Genesis Block (2009):** The first block, known as the Genesis Block or Block 0, was mined by Nakamoto in January 2009, marking the beginning of the blockchain as we know it today.

The Rise of Ethereum and Smart Contracts (2013-2015)

- **Ethereum's Introduction (2013):** Vitalik Buterin, a programmer and co-founder of Bitcoin Magazine, published a white paper proposing Ethereum. It aimed to build on the blockchain concept with a scripting language for developing more complex applications.

---

[1] https://bitcoin.org/bitcoin.pdf

- **Smart Contracts:** Ethereum's significant contribution was the idea of a 'smart contract', a programmable contract that executes automatically when conditions are met, without needing trusted intermediaries.

- **Network Launch (2015):** Ethereum went live in 2015, significantly expanding the potential applications of blockchain technology beyond cryptocurrency.

Expansion and Diversification (2016-Present)

- **Growing Interest and ICO Boom:** Post-2016 saw an explosion in the number of cryptocurrencies and the rise of Initial Coin Offerings (ICOs) as a means of crowdfunding for blockchain projects.

- **Enterprise Adoption:** Major corporations and consortia, like IBM and R3, began exploring blockchain for applications in finance, supply chain management, and more.

- **Non-Fungible Tokens (NFTs):** The concept of NFTs gained traction, allowing blockchain technology to be applied in art, music, and digital ownership.

- **Decentralized Finance (DeFi):** The rise of DeFi platforms further showcased blockchain's potential in transforming financial services by enabling lending, borrowing, and trading without traditional financial intermediaries.

Challenges and Future Trends

- **Scalability Issues:** As blockchain technology gained popularity, scalability became a significant challenge, particularly for networks like Bitcoin and Ethereum.

- **Energy Consumption:** The Proof of Work (PoW) consensus mechanism, mainly used by Bitcoin, has been criticized for its high energy consumption.

- **Regulatory Landscape:** The rise of cryptocurrencies and blockchain applications has prompted governments and regulatory bodies to consider and implement regulatory frameworks.

- **Emerging Solutions:** In response to these challenges, new technologies and concepts are emerging, including Proof of Stake (PoS), sharding, layer-2 solutions, and more.

- **Interoperability and Integration:** Efforts are underway to enable interoperability between blockchains and integrate blockchain technology into other sectors.

As blockchain continues to evolve, it is becoming increasingly clear that its potential extends beyond just powering cryptocurrencies. Its foundational principles of decentralization, immutability, and transparency can revolutionize various aspects of business, governance, and individual rights to privacy and ownership.

APPENDIX: A BRIEF HISTORY OF ARTIFICIAL INTELLIGENCE

The history of Artificial Intelligence (AI) is a fascinating journey through a landscape of ideas, discoveries, and aspirations. It's a field where philosophy, mathematics, engineering, and neuroscience converge to understand and emulate intelligence through machines. Here's a detailed look at its evolution:

The Early Years: Philosophical Foundations and Initial Theories (1940s-1950s)

- **Formative Ideas:** The idea of artificial intelligence begins with ancient myths and stories of artificial beings endowed with intelligence or consciousness by master craftsmen. Philosophers like Aristotle and Descartes planted early seeds of thought about the human mind and automation.

- **Turing Test (1950):** Alan Turing, a British polymath, proposed the Test in his paper "Computing Machinery and Intelligence", setting a fundamental goal and vision for AI:

creating machines that could mimic human intelligence convincingly.

- **First AI Programs (1950s):** The 1950s saw the development of the first programs that could perform tasks requiring intelligence. These included the Logic Theorist (1955) by Allen Newell and Herbert A. Simon and the checker-playing program by Arthur Samuel.

Early Optimism and the First AI Winter (1960s-1970s)

- **AI Research and Funding:** AI research gained momentum in the 1960s, with significant interest and funding, particularly in the United States and the United Kingdom. Early AI research focused on symbolic methods and problem-solving.

- **Initial Successes:** Early successes in AI included natural language processing and robotics. ELIZA (1966), an early natural language processing computer program, and Shakey the robot (late 1960s) are notable examples.

- **The First AI Winter (1970s):** AI research hit its first major setback, known as the "AI Winter", due to inflated expectations, limited computational power, and a lack of sophisticated algorithms. Funding and interest in AI significantly waned.

A Renewed Focus: Expert Systems and the Second AI Winter (1980s-1990s)

- **Rise of Expert Systems:** The 1980s saw a revival of interest in AI with the development of expert systems designed to mimic the decision-making ability of a human expert. They were used in industries for various applications.

- **Japan's Fifth Generation Computer Project:** Launched in 1982, this ambitious project aimed to create a new class of computers to implement AI applications. However, it eventually fell short of its goals.

- **The Second AI Winter (Late 1980s-1990s):** AI faced another period of reduced funding and interest towards the end of the 1980s, partly due to the limitations of expert systems and the failure of the Fifth-Generation project.

The Emergence of Modern AI: Machine Learning and Deep Learning (2000s-Present)

- **Rise of Machine Learning:** In the late 1990s and 2000s, AI shifted towards data-driven approaches with the advent of the internet and an explosion in data. Machine learning, mainly through neural networks, began to show promising results.

- **Deep Learning Revolution (2010s):** The 2010s witnessed a surge in AI capabilities, mainly due to advancements in deep learning. The success of AlexNet in 2012 at the ImageNet competition was a pivotal moment.

- **AI in Everyday Life:** AI applications have become a part of everyday life, from voice assistants like Siri and Alexa to recommendations on Netflix and YouTube.

- **Ethical and Societal Implications:** As AI becomes more advanced and widespread, concerns about privacy, bias, job displacement, and ethical use have gained prominence.

Looking to the Future

- **Continued Advancements and Challenges:** AI continues to advance, tackling more complex tasks and integrating with various technologies like the Internet of Things (IoT) and blockchain.

- **Interdisciplinary Collaboration:** AI's future lies in collaboration with fields like neuroscience, cognitive science, and ethics, aiming for holistic growth and responsible use of AI.

From its early philosophical roots to its current status as a staple of modern technology, AI's history reflects humanity's enduring fascination with the idea of creating intelligence and the immense possibilities that lie ahead.

MORE BOOKS BY THE AUTHOR

Thought-Provoking Quotes & Reflections on Artificial Intelligence

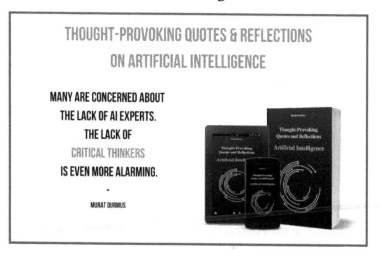

Available on Amazon (ISBN-13: 979-8857313763)

A PRIMER TO THE 42 MOST COMMONLY USED MACHINE LEARNING ALGORITHMS (WITH CODE SAMPLES)

The Cognitive Biases Compendium

Explore over 150 Cognitive Biases (with examples) to make better decisions, think critically, solve problems effectively, and communicate more accurately.

Available on Amazon (ISBN-13: 979-8851721496)

MINDFUL AI: Reflections on Artificial Intelligence

- ISBN-13: 979-8360396796

INSIDE ALAN TURING: QUOTES & CONTEMPLATIONS

- ISBN-13: 979-8751495848

RUMI - Drops of Enlightenment: (Quotes & Poems)

- ISBN-13: 979-8430816995

THE WISDOM OF MARCUS AURELIUS: Selected Thoughts and Quotes for a Fulfilled Life

- ISBN-13: 979-8387254581

The Sharp Mind of Ludwig Wittgenstein: Selected Thoughts and Quotes

- ISBN-13: 979-8388654298

THOUGHT-PROVOKING QUOTES & CONTEMPLATIONS FROM FAMOUS PHYSICISTS

- ISBN-13: 979-8543952337